90

YOUR HEALTH

Health and Drugs

Dorothy Baldwin

Rourke Enterprises, Inc.
Vero Beach, FL 32964

Your Health

Health and Food
Health and Exercise
Health and Drugs
Health and Hygiene
Health and Feelings
Health and Friends

Some words in these books are
printed in **bold**. Their meanings
are explained in the glossary
on page 30.

First published in the
United States in 1987 by
Rourke Enterprises, Inc.
Vero Beach, FL 32964

Library of Congress Cataloging-in-Publication Data

Baldwin, Dorothy.
   Health and drugs.

   (Your health)   32 p. : col. ill.
   Bibliography: p.
   Includes index.
   Summary: Discusses the effects and dangers of tobacco, alcohol, and
such drugs as marijuana and other narcotics.
   1. Drug abuse—Physiological aspects—Juvenile literature. 2. Drugs—
Toxicology—Juvenile literature. [1. Smoking. 2. Alcohol. 3. Drugs.
3. 4. Drug abuse
   I. Title.   II. Series: Baldwin, Dorothy. Your health.
   RC564.B33 1987   616.86   87–12927
   ISBN 0–86592–292–6

Phototypeset by DP Press, Sevenoaks, Kent
Printed in Italy by Sagdos S.p.A. Milan

Contents

The choices you have to make 4

Smoking 5
Here are some figures 5
The risks you take 6
What are the drugs in tobacco? 6
The damage smoking does 7
Do your parents smoke? 10

Passive smoking 13
The effects of passive smoking 13

Drinking 14
"A little of what you fancy . . ." 14
"A lot of what you fancy . . ." 14
Amounts of alcohol 15
How much can people drink? 15
How alcohol works 16
Alcohol and road accidents 18

Drug abuse 21
The effect illegal drugs have 21
Cannibis 22
The solvents 23
The dangers of solvent abuse 24
The narcotics 25
Drug pushers and young people 26

Drug abuse is rare 27
Why do a few young people start
taking drugs? 28
Help for those who misuse drugs 28
Your life! Your health! Your choice! 29

Glossary 30

Further reading 31

Index 32

The choices you have to make

This book is about drugs. It is also about the choices people have to make, particularly young people. For example, will you choose to look after your health and stay away from drugs? Or will you choose to ignore your health? You cannot make proper choices unless you know all the facts. This book will give you the information you need to help you to make your own decisions.

During your life you will have to make many choices, a lot of them when you are still quite young. Will you make the choices that will keep you healthy now and for your future life?

Will you choose health?

Smoking

Tobacco should be studied first, because it is the drug that causes most damage to young people. For every thousand teenagers who smoke, on average:

- Six will be killed on the roads.
- Two hundred and fifty will be killed before their time by smoking.

Tobacco also comes first because it is at your age that a few young people begin to smoke in secret out of curiosity.

Young people often try smoking because they are curious. Studies have shown that each cigarette reduces the smoker's life by five minutes.

Here are some figures

When questioned about their experience of smoking, people gave the following answers:

- 95 percent of people said smoking made their eyes sting.
- 50 percent said it gave them a runny nose.
- 45 percent said they coughed and wheezed for some time.
- 40 percent coughed up phlegm from their lungs.

Other side effects that were described were getting a headache, feeling dizzy, wanting to vomit and having an upset stomach. Do you think it is still worth having a try?

Cigarette smoke is made up of many substances dangerous to health, including nicotine, tar *and* carbon monoxide.

The risks you take

Tobacco is made up of very powerful drugs. All drugs affect the body and the mind. Once they have started taking drugs, people need more and more of them. Soon, those who are smokers start to crave (have extreme longing for) cigarettes. They cannot give up smoking. This is called **addiction**, and the people are called **addicts**. Many studies have been carried out on teenage smoking. The results all showed that people who smoke only two or three cigarettes when they are young have a 70 percent chance of smoking for the rest of their lives! That seems incredible! But it is true. The drugs in tobacco smoke are so powerful that they quickly make a person "hooked" for life.

What are the drugs in tobacco?

Tobacco smoke is a mixture of gases and tiny drops of moisture. There are several hundred different compounds (chemicals that combine) in the smoke. The ones that cause most damage are:

Nicotine – This is the main cause of addiction. The smoke is breathed into the lungs. The nicotine passes into the blood. It can reach the brain within five seconds! Nicotine causes an instant dizzy, sick feeling. It is then sent around the body, where it causes health problems. At the same time, the brain is urging the smoker to supply more nicotine.

Tar – This is a sticky and slightly gritty substance. You cannot see tar (or nicotine) as it is contained in tiny drops of moisture. The tar sticks to the delicate lining of the lungs and builds up into pools. The gritty part scratches the lining, irritating it and causing damage.

Carbon monoxide – This is also in the smoke you can see. (The tar and nicotine are in fine drops inside the smoke.) Carbon monoxide is a gas that can poison. It is taken by the blood to the heart, where it causes great damage.

The damage smoking does

Cancer – It is thought that about 80 percent of all cancers are caused by things that irritate the delicate parts inside the body. Anything that does this is called a **carcinogen** – a cancer-causing substance.

The tar in tobacco irritates the lungs and can cause lung cancer. Almost 90 percent of deaths from lung cancer are caused by smoking. However, not all smokers develop lung cancer.

There is a risk of developing cancer in the mouth and throat as the tar is breathed in. And, as the body gets rid of the tar by passing it in the urine, smokers also risk cancer of the bladder.

Heart disease – Nicotine makes the heart beat faster than it should. This puts a strain on the heart and on the blood vessels as well.

Carbon monoxide passes into the blood and cuts down the amount of oxygen it can carry.

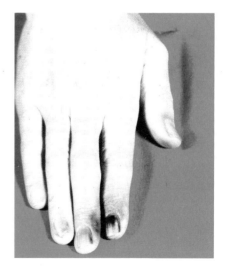

Smoking not only damages the inner parts of the body. It can also stain the teeth and fingers (shown here), making them unattractive.

This not only damages the heart; it also slows down the whole body. People need a lot of oxygen for sports, dancing, athletics and so on. Can you figure out why people who are good at activities that involve vigorous exercise do not smoke?

Bronchitis The breathing tubes are called **bronchi**. This is where the word for the illness bronchitis comes from. As the smoker coughs to get rid of the sticky tar, too much coughing damages the delicate lining of the bronchi and the smoker gets attacks of bronchitis. Over the years these attacks put a terrible strain on the heart and the lungs.

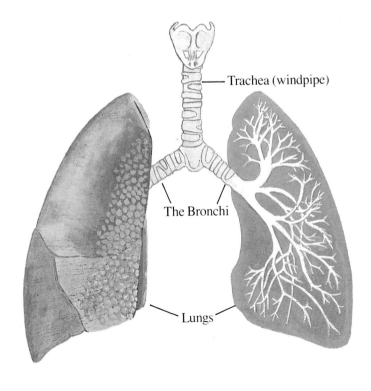

A diagram of the bronchi. *Heavy smokers usually have bad attacks of coughing that damage the delicate lining of the* bronchi.

Trachea (windpipe)

The Bronchi

Lungs

Other diseases – Smoking causes a great deal of damage to health in many ways. The stomach can be badly harmed. The legs and feet of a heavy smoker can "go bad" because:

● The blood vessels are too weak to carry enough blood to them.

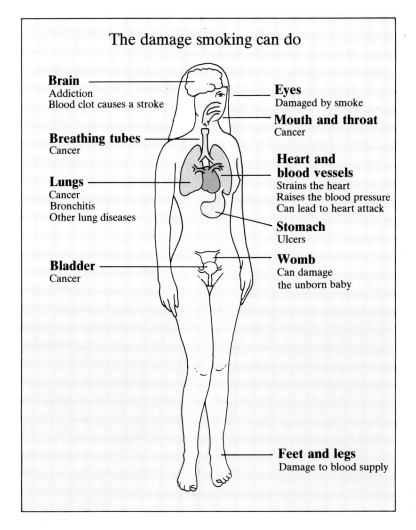

The damage smoking can do

Brain
Addiction
Blood clot causes a stroke

Eyes
Damaged by smoke

Mouth and throat
Cancer

Breathing tubes
Cancer

Heart and blood vessels
Strains the heart
Raises the blood pressure
Can lead to heart attack

Lungs
Cancer
Bronchitis
Other lung diseases

Stomach
Ulcers

Womb
Can damage
the unborn baby

Bladder
Cancer

Feet and legs
Damage to blood supply

This diagram shows the areas of the body that can be damaged by smoking.

● Not enough oxygen can reach them, because of the high levels of carbon monoxide in the blood.

In this case, the legs and feet "die" and a few very heavy smokers have had their legs amputated (cut off) because the damage was so bad.

Do your parents smoke?

Nearly all smokers want to stop smoking. But they find it very difficult. They are addicted to the drug. Do not blame your parents if they have become tobacco addicts, because when they first started smoking they did not know how dangerous it was. If they can manage to stop now, they will be able to get fit and healthy again, which is good news. But it may take quite a long time.

Smoking has a bad effect on performance in sports and exercise. Daley Thomson, the Olympic decathlon champion, refuses to smoke, or drink alcohol, *another drug.*

Many governments put a heavy tax on pipe, cigar and cigarette tobacco. This makes life very expensive for the smoker. Find out the price of a pack of cigarettes and then work out how much a smoker spends if seven packs are bought each week. Many governments also insist that a warning is put on each advertisement for cigarettes, and on each pack.

The wording below this advertisement for cigarettes reads: SMOKING CAN CAUSE LUNG CANCER, BRONCHITIS AND OTHER CHEST DISEASES. Government health warnings appear with all advertisements for brands of cigarettes. Do you think cigarettes should be advertised at all?

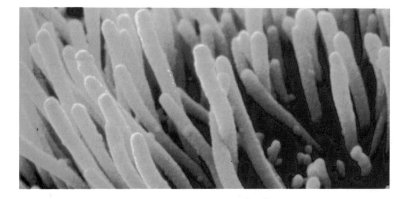

The lungs are lined with tiny hairs called cilia, which protect them from harmful substances. Here, on the right, you can see healthy cilia that have been magnified many times.

The cilia on the right have been destroyed by the tar in cigarette smoke. These cilia have been stained with a blue dye to help you see them better.

Passive smoking

Passive is a word that means that you are not doing anything, but that something is being done to you. Smokers pollute (make harmful) the air because they breathe out some of the carcinogens, nicotine and carbon monoxide from their cigarettes. If you are standing or sitting near a smoker, you breathe in all these things. You become a passive smoker. Do you think this is fair? Discuss with your friends whether you think smoking should be banned in public places.

Smokers not only put their own health at risk but also that of non-smokers who are forced to breathe in the same smoky air.

The effects of passive smoking

Studies have shown that those who are at risk from passive smoking are:

● Unborn babies: Mothers who smoke tend to have smaller babies than non-smoking mothers, and there is a greater risk of losing the baby before or soon after birth.

● Small children: The children of parents who smoke have more coughs, colds and chest complaints than the children of non-smoking parents.

● Other people: A non-smoker in a very smoky room breathes in the same amount of carcinogens in one hour as a smoker breathes in during several filter-tipped cigarettes.

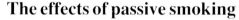

Can you say which of these are soft drinks and which contain alcohol? Can you think of some other drinks that contain alcohol?

Drinking

Look at the picture of the various types of drinks. Which are the soft drinks? Which of the drinks contain **alcohol**? Alcohol is a drug. In its natural form, alcohol is a colorless liquid derived from sugars that have undergone a chemical change. It changes the way people act and feel. If people drink a lot of alcohol, they may become addicted to the drug. These people are called **alcoholics**. It is a very difficult, frightening and painful process to give up alcohol once this stage has been reached.

"A little of what you fancy . . ."
Do you know this saying? The ending is ". . . does you good." A small amount of alcohol cheers some people up. After work, adults may like to relax with a drink. Younger people may be looking for excitement. They may hope to meet new friends. They have an alcoholic drink to help them to stop feeling nervous or a little shy.

"A lot of what you fancy . . ."
The ending of the saying is ". . . does you harm." The more alcohol a person drinks the more she or he is likely to become dependent.

Some adults say that one or two alcoholic drinks help them to relax.

Some people dislike alcohol. They take vows never to drink it. Other people find that even a small drink of alcohol makes them feel dizzy and sick. Because alcohol is a drug, and it is known that some people become addicted if they drink excessive amounts, certain religions have banned its use altogether.

Some religions forbid the drinking of alcohol *because of its effects. Here, Saudi Arabian Muslims will have soft drinks or water with their meal.*

Amounts of alcohol

There is the same amount of alcohol in one glass of wine, one small sherry, one half-pint of beer or lager and one ounce of hard liquor. Hard liquors includes whiskey, gin, vodka, rum and brandy. Each separate drink is called a **unit**.

How much can people drink?

In excess, alcohol damages the liver, the heart and the kidneys over a period of time. It also shrinks the brain. It has been worked out how much alcohol people can drink without causing damage to their health.

From left to right, these glasses contain whiskey, lager and wine. Each equals one unit *of* alcohol.

Maximum amount of alcohol that can be drunk safely	
Type of person	**Units of alcohol per day**
Men	four
Women	two
Expectant mothers (where there is a risk to unborn baby)	one

How alcohol works

Like all drugs, alcohol is quickly taken in the blood to the brain. It works in a cunning way. One unit is enough to "dampen down" the thinking and reasoning part of the mind. This is why people become more cheerful – they stop worrying about their problems.

After three units, drinkers cannot judge things very well. They cannot judge that they should stop drinking. They cannot judge road speeds and so become dangerous drivers, causing serious accidents.

After five units, the part of their brain that controls the drinkers' senses works very slowly. Heavy drinkers begin to talk in a jumbled, slurred way.

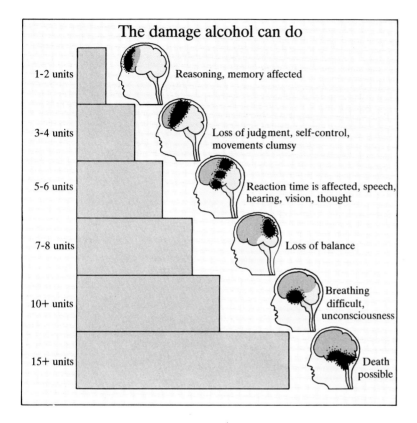

The damage alcohol can do

Units	Effect
1-2 units	Reasoning, memory affected
3-4 units	Loss of judgment, self-control, movements clumsy
5-6 units	Reaction time is affected, speech, hearing, vision, thought
7-8 units	Loss of balance
10+ units	Breathing difficult, unconsciousness
15+ units	Death possible

From this diagram you can see the effect increasing units of alcohol have on the mind and body.

After seven units, the drinkers start losing their balance. They may fall over and move with stumbling steps.

After ten units, they may pass out. They become unconscious because their brain has almost stopped working.

You may think "I know adults who drink heavily and they seem all right." This is because the brain can quickly become used to regular, heavy doses of alcohol. This is called **tolerance**, and develops with most drugs. When the brain can tolerate large amounts of the drug alcohol, the drinker needs more and more doses to experience the same effects.

Young people have no tolerance for alcohol. After a few drinks, they become very sick. If they go on drinking, they can behave in very violent ways. Taking risks, getting into fights and doing silly things that lead to crime are some of the things young drinkers can do.

Alcohol and road accidents

In all Western countries, it has been discovered that some people in their late teens are starting to drink heavily. Road accidents are the biggest

Many road accidents are caused by drivers who have drunk too much alcohol.

single killer of people between the ages of 15 and 24. Most of the accidents happen because reason and common sense are drugged by alcohol. For example:

● Pedestrians will suddenly dash out into the road, forgetting to watch for danger.

● Drivers of motorbikes and cars take terrible risks with their own – and other people's – lives (see page 16).

Alcohol destroys the brain cells. This man can no longer cope with everyday life.

Some facts about alcohol

1. Alcohol is the cause of a third of all deaths on the road.
2. Many innocent people are killed or crippled for life by drivers who drink.
3. At home, heavy drinkers start quarrels that may end in violent blows.
4. Outside, police and ambulances are called to deal with street fights.
5. Alcohol is the biggest and most serious of all the drug problems today.

HINTS TO HELP

● A little alcohol cheers people up; a lot makes them careless or cruel.

● Never drive if you have been drinking.

● Never travel with a heavy drinker.

● Governments put a legal limit on how much people can drink and still be safe to drive. Find out how many units this is.

● Remember, alcohol works in a cunning way. It builds up tolerance and then a craving for more until a person has become dependent.

● Do not let anyone "talk you into" having a drink. If you do not want one, say "no."

Drug abuse

Tobacco and alcohol are drugs. So are medicines from the doctor or pharmacist that make you well. Medical drugs are made up into a safe dose so that the person taking them does not become dependent. There is even a small amount of the drug caffeine in coffee and tea. All these are **legal drugs**.

The **illegal drugs** include **heroin, cocaine** and **cannabis**. If you take them, you break the law. You have committed a crime and you can be sent to prison or made to pay a fine.

Coffee and tea are refreshing drinks, but they contain small amounts of the drug caffeine, so do not drink too many cups.

The effect illegal drugs have

First the drug-taker feels restless. Then this is followed by a "high." This is a feeling of great happiness and pride. It is also called **euphoria**. Of course, it is a false feeling. As the drug's effect wears off, the person feels unhappy again – restless, irritable and very worried – until more of the drug can be taken.

Different drugs affect different people in different ways. Not everyone experiences a "high." For example, a nervous person can become more nervous. The effects of some drugs can be very frightening indeed. Objects can seem to change size or shape; time seems to

Some drugs have the effect of making ordinary objects appear in a strange and frightening way.

speed up or to stand still. The world of the drug-taker can turn into a nightmare where horrible things keep happening. This is called having a "bad trip." The drug-taker may panic and do something very dangerous because he or she is not in control of the mind.

Cannabis

The drug cannabis has many other names: marijuana, pot, hash, grass and ganga. Cannabis can be made up into little cakes and eaten. More often, it is smoked as a cigarette, and tobacco is mixed with it. The smoke has to

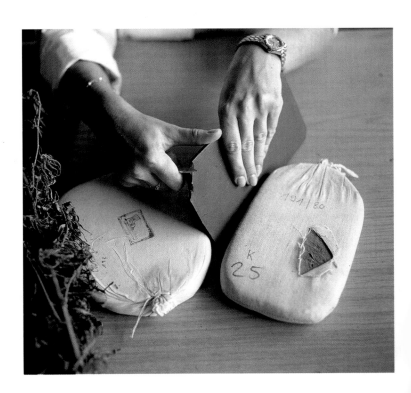

Cannabis comes from a bushy plant that grows wild in many parts of the world.

be breathed deep into the lungs. Cannabis smokers usually have a bad cough.

People who drink a lot of alcohol and smoke tobacco are more likely to try cannabis than those who do not. People who use cannabis are more likely to try "harder" drugs. Smoking cannabis can cause bronchitis, heart disease and lung cancer (see pages 7–8). Research is being carried out to find out the possible damage it causes to other parts of the body.

A young person may try cannabis just to see what it is like. If the person has a bad experience, he or she is not likely to try it again. But if the person enjoys feeling drugged, there is the risk he or she will keep wanting more. Cannabis smoking stops the mind working properly. A young person who uses it takes much longer to grow up mentally.

The solvents

Solvents are things put into glue, paint, nail polish remover and cleaning fluids to stop them from going hard. They are also used in aerosol spray cans and cigarette lighter fuels. If the solvent is sniffed or sprayed into the face it acts on the brain very quickly. Then the "sniffer" has a "high" and experiences a strange, floating feeling. It is rather like waking up after having an **anaesthetic**. Because the person feels strange, there is a risk he or she will act in unusual, often dangerous ways.

Close contact with solvents burns the skin, leaving painful sores.

The dangers of solvent abuse

To get a quicker "high" from the solvent, some people put a large plastic bag over their heads to keep out fresh air. This enables the sniffer to breathe in a stronger dose of the glue fumes or spray. Lack of oxygen may cause the sniffer to faint. Sniffers can die from lack of air. More often, they get sick inside the plastic bag as they faint. They may breathe their vomit into their lungs – and drown.

Some solvents make the heart beat too fast; the sniffer can die of a heart attack. Gases that are sprayed directly into the mouth can cause death because the throat swells up inside, and the person suffocates from lack of air.

Another very sad effect is that the person's brain can become damaged by the drug. Brain cells do not mend once they have been damaged. The person may become mentally handicapped for life.

Only a very, very small number of people abuse solvents. They are usually young, between the ages of 10 and 16. It is believed that more boys do this than girls.

People who abuse solvents are often having problems in their lives. But remember, any problem becomes worse by taking drugs, not better. The few young people who do abuse solvents are in urgent need of help before they do serious harm to themselves causing grief to families and friends.

Glue sniffing can have very sad results. The sniffer may faint and then vomit while unconscious, in some cases drowning in the vomit.

The narcotics

These include cannabis, heroin, morphine and cocaine. Narcotics are used by doctors to help deaden great pain. They can be swallowed, breathed in or injected. They cause a quick feeling of euphoria, followed by confusion, sleep, or fainting, depending on how much of the drug is taken. Heroin and morphine are called "hard" drugs, because a person taking them quickly develops tolerance, becomes dependent in mind and body, or may die from an overdose the first time they take the drug.

Drugs like **speed, barbiturates** and cocaine are very dangerous and cause more deaths than "hard drugs."

A young addict injects heroin *into his arm. Self-injecting is very dangerous because people may share needles and spread diseases. The incurable virus AIDS can be spread in this way.*

Drug pushers and young people

Illegal drugs can only be bought from drug pushers, who sell drugs unlawfully. They do their best to "push" or tempt people into taking drugs. They sell the drugs by the weight. They often add cheap things such as brick dust and cleaning powders to the drug to make up the quantity. It is easy to cheat young people this way. Drug pushers usually add lactose or glucose and other drugs to heroin because these give a "**rush**" to the brain, something heroin fails to do after people become dependent.

For this reason, drug-takers can never be sure what they are buying. Cheap things added to drugs are very dangerous to health. Sometimes, the drug pushers add lethal (deadly) poisons. Do you think the law is right to punish drug pushers very severely?

A drug pusher persuades two children to buy drugs. Drug dependence is expensive. It can make people steal and often leads to serious crime.

Drug abuse is rare

Only a tiny number of people abuse drugs. Young people need to remember this when they read dramatic newspaper articles about drug abuse among young people. It is easy to be impressed by newspaper stories and to think, "If everyone is trying drugs, why don't I?" But everyone is not taking drugs. The stories in the newspapers are often exaggerated. They are meant to frighten young people. Unfortunately, they sometimes have the opposite effect.

Only you can choose a healthy way of life for yourself.

Why do a few young people start taking drugs?

● Curiosity: "I wanted to see what it was like. I thought I could stop anytime I wanted."

● Pleasure: "It felt good. I liked being "high." I didn't realize how bad I'd feel when the drug wore off."

● Friends: "My friends told me I had to try. Now I'm a drug addict, they have stopped being my friends."

● Self-pity: "Nobody liked me, not even my parents. I thought they'd be sorry if I started taking drugs."

Help for those who abuse drugs

People who take drugs need help. It is easy to make mistakes when you are young. The really smart thing is to put your mistakes right. Adults know this and they are always ready to help. Some famous pop stars and celebrities, who were once drug addicts, now speak openly about how they were cured, hoping to stop their fans from taking drugs.

Once people decide to stop taking drugs, they immediately start to get better. They may experience horrid feelings called **withdrawal symptoms** — being shaky, sick and very ill. But withdrawal symptoms show that the body and mind are getting rid of the effects of the drug. Soon the addict will recover normal health and become much happier.

Your life! Your health! Your choice!

When you were very young, people looked after your health. Now you are growing up, you have to be able to look after yourself. Only you can make choices about drugs and your health. Do you think any of the reasons why people begin to take drugs like cannabis and heroin apply to smoking and alcohol? You might like to talk about this with your friends. Nobody can force you to make unhealthy choices unless you really want to. The decision lies with you.

In 1986, Nancy Reagan, wife of the President, began a campaign to persuade children to say "no" to drugs.

Glossary

Addiction The overpowering need that people taking drugs have to supply themselves with more of the particular drug. They are **addicts**. It is psychological plus physical dependence.

Alcohol This comes from sugars that have undergone chemical changes. It affects the body and the mind. Heavy drinkers who become addicted are called **alcoholics.**

Anaesthetic Powerful painkiller that puts a person to sleep.

Barbiturates Strong drugs, used in medicine to bring about sleep.

Bronchitis An infection of the breathing tubes, called **bronchi**.

Cancer An abnormal growth of cells in one or more organs of the body.

Cannabis A drug taken from the marijuana plant. It can be smoked or eaten.

Carbon monoxide A dangerous gas produced by **tobacco**.

Carcinogen Any substance that causes **cancer**, by irritating delicate body organs.

Cocaine It is a white powder. It makes people feel "high" for a short time. Then they cannot eat, sleep or keep still because they feel awful. They do not become physically dependent on it. **Cocaine** can cause sudden death.

Dependence The overpowering need to take a drug in ever-increasing doses.

Euphoria A false feeling of pride and great happiness produced by drugs for a short period, followed by unhappiness until the next dose is taken.

Heart disease Disease that affects the heart's ability to pump blood around the body.

Heroin One of the "hard" drugs. People become dependent on it very quickly.

Illegal drugs Use of these drugs has been forbidden by governments because they are very dangerous. Selling or using them leads to imprisonment or a fine. They include **narcotics, cannabis, LSD, solvents** and "**speed.**"

Legal drugs They include **nicotine, alcohol** and **caffeine** (in coffee) and can be freely taken by law, although there are government warnings about them.

Morphine One of the **narcotic** drugs, used in medicine as a powerful painkiller.

Oxygen A gas that is vital to life.

Narcotics These are painkillers and include **heroin, morphine** and **cocaine**.

Nicotine A colorless substance in **tobacco**. It is very addictive.

"Rush" The feeling produced when a substance injected into a vein reaches the brain. Objects seem to "whizz" upward.

Solvents Substances put in glue, paint and other objects to stop them from hardening. If "sniffed" they give a feeling of dizziness and a "high."

"Speed" One of the group of drugs called amphetamines, which gives a "high." It is very dangerous.

Tar A sticky, gritty substance produced by **tobacco**.

Tobacco Leaves of the **tobacco** plant, smoked as cigarettes, cigars or in a pipe.

Tolerance When the brain and body become used to regular heavy doses of a drug, such as **alcohol**, and need more of the drug to gain the same effect.

Unit A measure of a drink, based on how much **alcohol** that quantity contains.

Withdrawal symptoms Feelings experienced when a person stops taking a particular drug he or she has come to need. They can include sickness, epileptic fits, headaches and fear.

Further reading

Berger, Gilda. *Addiction: Its Causes, Problems, and Treatments*. Watts, 1982.

Cohen, Miriam. *Marijuana, Its Effects on Mind and Body*. Chelsea House, 1985.

Cohn, Susan. *A Six-Pack and a Fake I.D.: Teens Look at the Drinking Problem*. Evans, M & Co., 1986.

Graeber, Laurel. *Are You Dying for a Drink? Teenagers and Alcohol Abuse*. Messner, 1985.

Hyde, Margaret O. *Know About Smoking*. McGraw-Hill, 1983.

Hyde, Margaret O. *Mind Drugs*. (5th edition) Dodd Mead, 1986.

Sonnett, Sherry. *Smoking*. Watts, 1977.

Woods, Geraldine. *Drug Use and Drug Abuse*. Watts, 1986.

Picture Acknowledgments

The Publisher would like to thank the following for providing pictures for the book: Abdul Latif Al Hoad 15; Cameratalks 6, 7, 12 (above and below), 13, 21, 23, 24; John Hillelson Agency Ltd 29; Tim Humphrey 14 (below); Malcolm Walker 4, 9, 17; Tim Woodcock cover, 11, 14 (above), 15, 26; Zefa 5, 18, 19, 22, 25, 27; the remainder are from the Wayland Picture Library.

Index

Addiction, 6, 20, 21
Addicts, 6, 9
Alcohol, 14–18, 20, 21,
  23, 29
Alcoholics, 14
Amputation, 9

Blood, 7, 9, 16
Body, 8, 23, 25, 28
Brain, 6, 15, 16, 17, 24
Breathing, 13, 22, 23, 24,
  25
Bronchi, 8
Bronchitis, 8, 23

Caffeine, 21
Cancer, 7
  of the bladder, 7
  of the lung, 7, 23
  of the mouth, 7
  of the throat, 7
Cannabis, 21, 22, 23, 25,
  29
Carbon monoxide, 7, 10
Carcinogen, 7, 13
Cigarettes, 6, 10, 13, 22
Cocaine, 21, 25
Cough, 5, 8, 13, 23
Curiosity, 5, 28

Dangerous drivers, 16,
  19
Dependence, 14, 25, 26

Drug pushers, 26
Drug-takers, 21, 22
Drugs, 4, 6, 12, 16, 17,
  25–29
  illegal, 21, 22, 23, 25,
    26
  legal, 21
  abuse of, 21–29

Euphoria, 21, 25

Gases, 6, 7
Glue sniffing, 23, 24
Government health
  warnings, 10, 20

Hard drugs, 23, 25
Heart, 6, 7, 8, 15, 24
  disease, 7, 23
Heroin, 21, 25, 26, 29
"High," 21, 23, 24

Liver, 15
Lungs, 5, 6, 7, 8, 23, 24

Marijuana, 22
Medicines, 21
Mind, 6, 16, 23, 25, 28

Narcotics, 25
Newspaper reports, 27
Nicotine, 6, 7

Overdose, 25
Oxygen, 7, 10, 24

Passive smoking, 13
People who will help, 28

Road accidents, 5, 16, 18,
  19, 20
"Rush," 26

Safe amounts of alcohol,
  16
Smoking, 5–13, 22, 23, 29
Solvent abuse, 23, 24
Speed, 25
Spirits, 15

Tar, 7, 8
Tobacco, 5, 6, 10, 12, 21,
  22
  compounds, 6
Tolerance, 17, 18, 20, 25
"Trip," 21, 22

Unit of alcohol, 15–17, 20

Violence, 18, 20

Withdrawal symptoms,
  28